Being different

Exodus 33:1–17

'What else will distinguish me and your people from all the other people on the face of the earth?' (v.16b)

'Being diff
want – i
or an ou
to blend in so that
characterised by w
same language, adopting like ways of doing things and sharing beliefs. The Israelites also wanted to be like the nations around them, worshipping a god who could be seen, rather than Yahweh; so they fashioned a golden calf from their jewellery and worshipped it. Moses, returning from 40 days on the mountain top with God, is furious. He grinds the calf into a powder and makes the people drink it! God is also angry and threatens to withdraw His presence. But note that His promise of a land flowing with milk and honey and victory over their enemies still stands.

So why did Moses say that they weren't going anywhere without God Himself? Surely it was enough still to be known as God's people, still to be on the right road, still to be assured of victory and even to have an angel accompany them? No! Moses knew that the only thing that distinguishes God's people is His presence – nothing else will do.

As God's people we have the privilege of being 'different' – in the world but not of it (see John 17:16). Yet the same truth still holds – only God's presence in our lives will distinguish us from our non-believing neighbours. This month we will explore what is meant by God's presence, why it is so important, and how we can increasingly hear, like Moses, the promise 'My Presence will go with you' (Exod. 33:14). And when we do, nothing will ever be the same!

For prayer and reflection

Lord, You spoke with Moses face to face. May I seek Your friendship and desire the difference it makes. Amen.

WEEKEND

Seeking His face

For reflection: Psalm 27:1–4

'My heart says of you, "Seek his face!" Your face, LORD, I will seek.' (v.8)

The automatic door from the arrivals hall opened and I emerged, trailing my suitcase. I scanned the sea of humanity in front of me, looking for one face. There he was! My brother, whom I hadn't seen for over a year, was smiling and waving. Yes, we had tracked the details of each other's lives via email or text, but looking into his face was different.

The biblical writers express the concept of God's presence by speaking of His 'face'. When we see someone's face we encounter their immediate presence as opposed to the more indirect written word. As David declares his intent to seek God's face, he is committing himself to pursue a depth of intimacy and understanding with God beyond that which he has already experienced.

Brother Lawrence, a monk in the seventeenth century, expressed the same desire: 'I make it my priority to persevere in His holy presence, wherein I maintain a simple attention for God … it is an habitual, silent, and private conversation of the soul with God.'*

Spend time this weekend really noticing people's faces – what do you see?

Optional further reading

*Brother Lawrence, *The Practice of the Presence of God* (Oxford: One World Publications, 1993).

BEVERLEY SHEPHERD

Beverley is a trainer, writer and executive coach. She specialises in the areas of leadership, team development and stress management. One of her passions is the encouraging and equipping of Christians in the workplace and in 2011 she established PrayerWorks on behalf of LICC. A regular speaker at conferences and on the CWR Women's Weekends, Beverley has written several books including 'Insight into Stress' and 'Created as a Woman'.

FIONA VEITCH SMITH

Fiona Veitch Smith is a writer, editor and university lecturer living in Newcastle upon Tyne. She was born in Northumberland, but grew up in South Africa, where she became a Christian at age 11. Soon after getting married, she and her husband Rodney worked with Youth With A Mission in Cape Town, where they ran a Christian performing arts company and helped lead short-term outreach teams into Southern Africa. After leaving YWAM she worked as a journalist for both the Christian and secular media. Now that she's back in the UK, Fiona works part-time and looks after her young daughter. She and her family are active members of Heaton Baptist Church. You can get to know Fiona more at http://fiona.veitchsmith.com

 Published by CWR, Waverley Abbey House, Waverley Lane, Farnham, Surrey GU9 8EP, UK. Tel: 01252 784700 Email: mail@cwr.org.uk Registered Charity No. 294387. Registered Limited Company No. 1990308.
Front cover image: Getty/Echo. Concept development, editing, design and production by CWR. Printed in England by Linney Print.

Inspiring Women Every Day

MAR/APR 2013

March

THE PRESENCE OF GOD

BEVERLEY SHEPHERD

April

ECCLESIASTES: SEARCHING FOR MEANING

FIONA VEITCH SMITH

Plus … Special Article, Ministry Report and CWR Events Page

CWR

In **hiding**

Genesis 1:26–31; 3:6–11

'… and they hid from the LORD God among the trees of the garden.' (Gen. 3:8)

A friend was showing me a recent purchase – a beautiful (and expensive) skirt. 'I don't think I'll mention to Greg how much it cost', she commented. I fully understood that husband Greg might not recognise the true value of such an item! A harmless bit of 'hiding'? We hide all sorts of things – an empty chocolate wrapper, facts about ourselves, uncomfortable feelings, our precious belongings … but why do we do it? Reasons vary, but usually there is a mixture of fear and shame. These same reasons can cause us, like Adam and Eve, to hide from God. Perhaps we are ashamed of our actions or thoughts, or fearful of His interference in the running of our lives. If so, the thought of God's presence can seem more like a threat than a promise, not dissimilar to the 'Wait until your father gets home' warning issued by an exasperated mum.

Yet we were made to live in God's loving presence – to walk with Him in the cool of the day and know a deep and intimate relationship with the Father who created us in His own image. It's what we were born for! Scholars differ on the length of time Adam enjoyed this relationship – was it months, years, or decades that separated Genesis 1 and 3? However long, the sad truth is that once ended through sin, there was no going back – the way into the Garden was barred (Gen. 3:24). As the storyline of the Bible unfolds we see God's continued desire to dwell with His people and the reality of our sin causing a barrier between us and our holy God.

For prayer and reflection

Father, when You desire to walk with me in the cool of the day, may I be ready and eager to spend time with You. Bring into the light anything I may wish to hide.

TUES **MAR 5**

God's desire

Revelation 21:1–6; Psalm 33:18–22

'Now the dwelling of God is with men, and he will live with them … and be their God.' (Rev. 21:3)

Many years ago I read a helpful book on relationships. One particular phrase caught my attention: 'Love does not mean being a doormat and letting the other person walk all over you.' The author explained that, at times, love has to be tough. God exhibits this tough love. His desire, ever since sin entered the world and we were banished from the Garden, is to restore face-to-face intimacy with His people. But true intimacy can only take place in the context of faithfulness – hence 'the eyes of the LORD range throughout the earth to strengthen those whose hearts are fully committed to him' (2 Chron. 16:9).

The Bible ends with a picture of the New Jerusalem – a place where the intimacy of the Garden is fully restored and God dwells with His people. Between Genesis and Revelation is the amazing story of God's tough love inviting His people into that place of intimacy; the story of God's sacrificial love in giving His Son to die for us so that we can be reconciled to Him; and the story of His everlasting love wooing us: 'I have drawn you with loving-kindness' (Jer. 31:3). Yet His love is also protective and so throughout the Old Testament we see Him withdrawing His presence from His people, knowing that in their sinful state they could not see His face and live (Exod. 33:3).

God's desire for intimacy with His people has never wavered, but He is no doormat. This treasure is not available to those who are satisfied with a casual acquaintance with God. Yet the promise still remains that He will be found by those who seek Him with all their hearts – those who wholeheartedly long for His presence.

For prayer and reflection

Lord, may I know Your loving eyes upon me today, strengthening me. I desire that my heart be fully committed to You.

Hide or seek?

Exodus 20:1–3, 18–26

'The people stayed at a distance, while Moses approached the thick darkness where God was.' (v.21)

The clouds threatened rain, the wind was cold and, to have a good view, you had to get there early and be prepared for hours of waiting. Yet I was there! The opportunity to witness the historic river pageant celebrating Queen Elizabeth's Diamond Jubilee and watch her go past was not to be missed! Some friends, who had watched the event on TV in comfort, mediated through the BBC presenters, had questioned my choice. I did not!

The King of kings gives us a choice, and He does so to test us. How much do we desire intimacy with Him? It will not always be comfortable; it may involve waiting; it may be difficult to get a clear 'view' as other things crowd in to distract. When we step into the thick darkness as Moses did we are letting go of all control; we are laying down any agenda; we are confronting our fear. The Israelites feared that if they got too close to God they would die – and there is a dying that happens in the presence of the King. As C.S. Lewis puts it: 'Christ says, "Give me All. I don't want so much of your time and so much of your money and so much of your work: I want You. I have not come to torment your natural self, but to kill it. No half-measures are any good."'* Yet Moses made his choice – he wanted to be 'where God was'. And God honoured his choice: 'the LORD would speak to Moses face to face, as a man speaks with his friend' (Exod. 33:11). The Israelites made their choice – to stay at a 'safe' distance and not have God speak to them, except through Moses. And God accepted their choice.

God will accept our choice too – to hide from Him, or to seek Him.

*C.S. Lewis, *Mere Christianity*, copyright © C.S. Lewis Pte. Ltd. 1942, 1943, 1944, 1952.

For prayer and reflection

Lord, please forgive me when I have stayed at a distance from You and been satisfied with a relationship mediated through others.

THURS **MAR 7**

Hungry for blessing

Genesis 32:7–12, 21–32

'... I saw God face to face, and yet my life was spared.' (v.30b)

Now I know that you are not meant to covet, and yet I did. The longer she spoke the more evident it became that she had a depth of relationship with God and an ear tuned to His voice that was beyond my experience. It was also evident that she had given priority to seeking God's presence. Maybe covet is the wrong word – hunger might better describe my sense of there being much more of God to know and enjoy.

The Bible stories of those who encountered God face to face evoke just such a hunger, and together we will spend the next few days exploring these accounts, beginning with Jacob.

Jacob's meeting with God was far from comfortable – he wrestled with 'the man', refusing to let him go until he had received a blessing. Jacob had always been hungry for blessing – scheming to receive the blessing due to the elder son, his brother Esau, whereas 'Esau despised his birthright' (Gen. 25:34). So, did the night-long struggle mean that God was reluctant to bless Jacob? I don't believe so. It was obvious that God could disable Jacob at will and so end the wrestling match, yet He didn't. Somehow the struggle was part of the blessing! In it Jacob recognises that all his strategies for making life work (scheming, deception, manipulation) are of no avail; he is at the end of himself and totally dependent on the goodness of God. Only with that realisation can God give Jacob (the deceiver) a new name – Israel; only now can he become aligned with God's purposes for his life.

God is not reluctant to bless, but Jacob's example leaves me wondering if I sometimes let go too quickly. Am I hungry enough?

For prayer and reflection

Father, I ask for Jacob's tenacity and boldness. May I hold on to You and not let go, may I desire Your blessing as much as he did.

CWR MINISTRY EVENTS

Please pray for the team

DATE	EVENT	PLACE	PRESENTER(S)
1-3 Mar	Preparation for Marriage	Waverley Abbey House	Mick & Lynette Brooks with Andrew & Lynn Penson
2 Mar	Small Group Leaders' Toolbox	WAH	Andy Peck
8 Mar	God Unannounced	WAH	Andy Peck
11-15 Mar	Pastoral Care in the Local Church	WAH	Stuart Pascall, Lynn Penson and Team
18-22 Mar	Introduction to Biblical Care and Counselling	WAH	Angie Coombes and Team
21 Mar	Insight Day: Helping Couples with Troubled Marriages	Pilgrim Hall	Heather & Ian Churchill
25 Mar	Passover Supper	PH	Elizabeth Hodkinson
26 Mar	Passover Supper	WAH	Elizabeth Hodkinson
4 Apr	Leading a Church in a Driven World	WAH	Andy Peck
6 Apr	Successfully Navigating the Teenage Years	WAH	Owen & Laura Ashley
9 Apr	Transformational Leadership	WAH	Coleen Jackson and Robin Precey
19 Apr	Counselling Enquirers' Event	PH	Counselling Team
24 Apr	Managing Conflict Creatively	WAH	Chris Ledger
25 Apr	The Bible in a Day	WAH	Andy Peck
26-28 Apr	Women's Weekend: 'Springs of Life'	WAH	Nicky-Sue Terry and Ros Derges
2 May	Small Group Leaders' Evening	WAH	Andy Peck
7-9 May	Bible Discovery Weekend: 'The Pebble Who Became a Rock'	PH	Philip Greenslade
11 May	Understanding Yourself, Understanding Others (MBTI® Basic)	WAH	Andrew & Lynn Penson
28 May - 1 Jun	The Big Story	WAH	Philip Greenslade

Please also pray for students and tutors on our ongoing **BA in Counselling** programme at Waverley and Pilgrim Hall and our **Certificate and Diploma of Christian Counselling** and **MA in Integrative Psychotherapy** held at London School of Theology.

For further details and a full list of CWR's courses, phone +44 (0)1252 784719 or visit the CWR website at www.cwr.org.uk

FRI **MAR 8**

More!

Exodus 33:18–34:8

'Then Moses said, "Now show me your glory."' (v.18)

A little boy, holding out his empty bowl, daringly asks for more food on behalf of all the hungry children in the workhouse. He is punished. And so the orphaned Oliver Twist, in Charles Dickens' story, learns that hungering for more is unwise.

Not so in God's kingdom, where asking for 'more' is applauded, as the story of Moses illustrates. No man had encountered God in the ways Moses had. He responded to God's call at the burning bush, where God revealed the name which expresses His character: 'I AM WHO I AM.' Then, as Moses confronted Pharaoh he saw God's power at work in miraculous ways. In the Israelites' escape from Egypt he witnessed the parting of the Red Sea, water from the rock, daily provision of manna, and God's guidance by the pillars of cloud and fire. Surely he should have been satisfied? No! Moses asks for more: 'Now show me your glory'. This is no longer the Moses who pleads with God to send someone else (Exod. 4:13); he has been changed. As he has repeatedly stepped forward into God's presence, met with Him on the mountain, and challenged His intentions on behalf of the Israelites, he increasingly knows what it is to speak with God as a friend (Exod. 33:11). And God agrees to his request and shows him His glory – the unveiling of God's very being and nature, who He is. Central to God's nature is His goodness – He defines what goodness is. And Moses sees the goodness of the Lord who is compassionate and gracious, slow to anger and abounding in love and faithfulness (Psa. 103:8).

So, like Oliver, let's take our empty bowls and ask for more, knowing that in doing so we will hear the applause of heaven.

For prayer and reflection

O compassionate and gracious God, slow to anger and abounding in love, thank You that there are so many evidences of Your goodness in my life. Amen.

WEEKEND

Eat and get hungry

For reflection: Psalm 42:1–11

'My soul thirsts for God, for the living God. Where can I go and meet with God?' (v.2)

In the physical realm we get hungry by not eating. The spiritual realm is different – our hunger grows *through* eating! Hunger and thirst are key to maturity in the Christian life. The psalmist pictures himself not as a camel, self-sufficiently wandering the desert with its water-filled humps, but as a deer whose very life is dependent on finding streams.

Again and again God addresses His promises to the hungry. He 'satisfies the thirsty and fills the hungry with good things' (Psa. 107:9). Just as a mother's ear is tuned to the cry of her hungry baby, God's attention is drawn by our thirst for Him. Too often we have jaded our appetite by consuming junk food, be it mindless TV, romantic novels, computer games or pre-occupation with work, leading to spiritual stagnation and listlessness.

So let's take some time this weekend to stock up our spiritual larder with things to make us hungry – be it Bible passages, helpful talks, insightful books, prayer, worship or time with hungry friends – and let's plan our meals for the week ahead.

Optional further reading

Psalm 107:1–9; Matthew 5:1–12; Psalm 34:8–16.

MON **MAR 11**

The **meeting point**

Exodus 40:1–11, 34–38

'Then the cloud covered the Tent of Meeting, and the glory of the LORD filled the tabernacle.' (v.34)

A large sign was suspended from the ceiling in the busy airport arrivals area. It read 'Meeting Point'. Here families could re-connect, friends link up and business colleagues find each other. In our passage we see God establishing a meeting point, the tabernacle – a place where His presence would dwell amongst His people. In bringing the Israelites out of Egypt this was His goal: 'so that I might dwell among them' (Exod. 29:46). So important was this to Him that He gave Moses the exact blueprint for the tabernacle, specifying every detail. And His presence was tangible – represented by the cloud by day and fire by night. In His presence His people would learn His ways and the holiness that would distinguish them from all other nations.

But because of sin His presence required specific safeguards to protect the people from His consuming holiness. To even approach the Tent of Meeting you had to go via the altar of burnt offering and the laver. The altar was the place of sacrifice. Today, we no longer offer lambs and grain; instead 'a broken and contrite heart, O God, you will not despise' (Psa. 51:17). The laver, or bronze basin, was made of the women's mirrors and filled with water for washing. Entering God's presence requires preparation: 'Come near to God and he will come near to you. Wash your hands, you sinners, and purify your hearts, you double-minded' (James 4:8). Yet these safeguards were not designed to keep His people out, but to ensure that His presence could be enjoyed when they entered in. David would later sing 'you will fill me with joy in your presence' (Psa. 16:11).

For prayer and reflection

Thank You, Lord, that, despite my sinfulness, You have made a way for me to meet with You. May I prepare by coming to You via the altar and the laver.

Presumption

1 Samuel 4:1–11; Deuteronomy 11:22–25

'Let us bring the ark of the LORD's covenant from Shiloh, so that it may go with us and save us ...' (v.3)

The dictionary defines presumption as 'taking for granted'. It well describes the Israelites' attitude to God. Following on from their entry into the promised land and the death of Joshua, Israel had been led by a series of judges. The ark, symbolising God's presence with His people, had been installed at Shiloh, which became the central focus for worship. Yet worship had become ritual as 'everyone did as he saw fit' (Judg. 21:25b). Their own desires had become their god. They assumed, because of the ark, that God was with them and would bless them; they saw no need to observe God's command to 'love the LORD your God, to walk in all his ways and to hold fast to him ...' (Deut. 11:22). The Israelites ignored the need for true relationship, contenting themselves with the mere symbol of God's presence. It was only when the presence of the ark failed to deliver victory in battle that the truth of their situation was revealed: they were no different from the pagan nations surrounding them!

There is a tension in our Christian walk between a right assurance of our adoption as God's beloved children and His care for us, and the presumption that sees no need to develop our relationship with Him. Relationships take time and it may seem like there isn't enough time for everything on our 'to do' lists. But, as one wise monk pointed out to me, time is never really the issue – we always make time for those we love. If we love the Lord, we will want to walk in His ways and hold fast to Him, but it involves relinquishing the mindset that wants to do only as *we* see fit! Let's not take Him for granted!

For prayer and reflection

Lord, please forgive me when I take You for granted and presume on Your love without offering mine.

On **our terms**

1 Chronicles 13:1–14; 1 Chronicles 15:1–3,13–15

'We did not enquire of him [the Lord] about how to do it in the prescribed way.' (15:13)

Some years ago the song 'My Way' was made popular by Frank Sinatra – a song celebrating individualistic self-determination. It is the antithesis of Christian submission to the will of God and yet it easily infects our thinking and attitudes. We even seek to do God's work our way!

David was no different. He longed for the ark of God to be housed in a place of honour in Jerusalem, yet God had given very clear instructions for its transportation – no one but the Levites could carry it. David did not ask God – instead he replicated the ways of the Philistines who had used a cart to send the ark back to Israel (1 Sam. 6:7). The results were disastrous.

There can be many reasons for this 'failure to enquire of the Lord' in our own lives. Often it is a mixture of time pressure, concern that we may not 'hear' His answer or perhaps even a reluctance to let God interfere with our plans! Asking God means letting go of control and allowing Him to guide us. It requires trust in His wisdom, His goodness and His desire to communicate with us. But how much of our lives are we to ask God about? Surely we don't need to bother Him with every little detail? Frank Laubach, a missionary in the Philippines, sought moment by moment surrender to God's leadership and discovered 'the sense of being led by an unseen hand which takes mine while another hand reaches ahead and prepares the way'.* He learned what it meant to enjoy God's presence on a continual basis and submit all his decisions, even the smallest, to Him. I'm inspired by his example and next week we will explore how to follow it.

*Frank Laubach, 'Letters by a Modern Mystic', quoted in *Devotional Classics* (London: Hodder & Stoughton, 1990) p.176.

For prayer and reflection

Father, I ask that I may stay conscious of Your presence throughout today and seek Your guidance and direction in every decision I make. Thank You. Amen.

Hosting God

Psalm 84:1–12

'Better is one day
in your courts
than a thousand
elsewhere;
I would rather be
a doorkeeper ...'
(v.10)

Yesterday's passage mentioned Obed-Edom, in whose house the ark of God remained for three months (1 Chron. 13:14). We know little about this time except that the Lord blessed his household and everything he had. Obed-Edom obviously knew how to host the presence of the Lord!

What does it mean for the Lord to bless? God instructed Aaron and his sons to bless Israel saying: 'The LORD bless you and keep you; the LORD make his face shine upon you and be gracious to you; the LORD turn his face toward you and give you peace' (Num. 6:24–26). God's blessing indicates His acceptance and favour and results in peace (shalom). Shalom is more than the absence of strife but a positive state of wellbeing. Which of us wouldn't want this for our household? And it all comes from His face. God's intention is that His people, the people called by His name (Num. 6:27), would seek His face and be recognised by the blessing of favour and peace in their lives.

And when the ark was moved to Jerusalem, Obed-Edom went with it! He was addicted to the presence of God; with the psalmist he might well have cried out, 'My soul yearns, even faints for the courts of the LORD; my heart and flesh cry out for the living God' (v.2). We are told that he became a gatekeeper (1 Chron. 16:38) in the tabernacle, ministering before the ark of the Lord. His ministry comprised of making petition, giving thanks and praising God (1 Chron. 16:4), showing us how to minister to the Lord too.

Many addictions are unhealthy, but addiction to the presence of God leads to favour and shalom as Obed-Edom found!

For prayer and reflection

Obed-Edom followed the presence of God to Jerusalem – how much would you allow your life to be disrupted in order to more fully experience the presence of God?

Family likeness

John 14:1–14

'Anyone who has seen me has seen the Father.' (v.9b)

Going through some old family photos, I came across one of my brother in his late teens. I blinked – it could so easily have been a photo of his teenage son (except, of course, for the red bell bottoms!).

Over the past weeks we have seen that God's presence is referred to as His face – but what does God's face look like? It looks like Jesus! He is 'the exact representation of his being' (Heb. 1:3), not merely a good likeness. He is *the* authentic representation of who God is – if you don't see it in Jesus then it's not in God and if you see it in Jesus then you can be sure that it is also in the Father. And just as God told Moses His name, 'I AM', expressing His character, so Jesus revealed His character in seven 'I am' statements. In today's reading He states: 'I am the way and the truth and the life' (v.6). He is the one and only way to the Father and the truth about God's nature is found in Him alone.

In response to Philip's request (v.8) Jesus says, in effect: 'Everything you have seen and heard in the last three years has shown you what My Dad is like. When you watched Me embrace the outcast, you saw that no one is outside of My Father's love. When I fed the 5,000, you understood that My Father's love is demonstrated in tangible ways. When I heal and deliver, you know that My Father is powerful to save. When I forgive as I forgave the paralytic and the woman caught in adultery, you know that My Father forgives your sins. And the words I speak are My Father's words. Look at me, Philip, and see the Father's face!'

In our final week we will explore who Jesus says He is.

For prayer and reflection

Jesus, thank You for showing us what the Father is like; that as we look at You we see Him.

WEEKEND

Search me

For reflection: Psalm 139:1–24

'O LORD, you have searched me and you know me.' (v.1)

The application form for a course I wanted to attend contained the question: 'How would your friends describe you?' I decided to ask them … As you can imagine, this exercise was not without some concern but I trusted my friends' honesty. When Jesus says 'I am', He has perfect self-knowledge – my friends' answers helpfully revealed that I did not!

In the presence of God we not only discover what He is like, we also learn about ourselves. He can show us our hearts, our thoughts and our offensive ways. Yet He shows us, not to condemn us but to bring into the light that which needs changing (v.12). The creative power that knit us together in our mother's womb is also available to re-create and change us into His likeness – His hand is there to guide us and hold us.

This weekend consider making a list of 'I am' statements about yourself and then bring them into the presence of God to be 'searched'. You may also want to ask trusted friends to indicate their agreement with each statement on a scale of 1–10.

Optional further reading

John 1:43–51; 4:1–30.

Be Equipped and Empowered to Help Others

Are you involved in ministry to women or do you feel drawn to the possibility in the future? Our Woman to Woman course may be just the thing for you!

This popular five-day residential course covers topics including:

- developing vision;
- goals and godly leadership;
- caring for hurting people;
- the role of the personality within relationships;
- identifying spiritual gifting

– all based on a solid biblical foundation.

Previous courses have seen women flying in from Canada, Borneo, South Africa and Europe, as well as travelling from all over the UK. Each has arrived with high expectations and left feeling 'equipped and empowered', and with a deeper sense of God's love and purpose for their lives and ministry.

Linda returned to Canada having enjoyed the quality of teaching in particular. She commented that the tutor 'inspired [her] to live with more trust, courage and joy', which she would carry back to her community in Didsbury, Alberta.

'This has been five days of physical and spiritual feasting'

Other delegates remarked upon the care they received, the inspirational and honest teaching, the opportunities to share with other women and the laughter amidst great food!

We hope you will join us this year, that you likewise may be equipped and empowered to help others.

Woman to Woman
Mon–Fri 17–21 June 2013
Pilgrim Hall, East Sussex
For more information/to book,
visit **www.cwr.org.uk/training**
Or call **+44 (0)1252 784719**

'A course for any woman with a heart to come alongside other women'

MON **MAR 18**

Time in His presence (1)

1 Kings 19:1–19

'Get up and eat, for the journey is too much for you.' (v.7)

Having spent time looking at people who have sought God's presence, are you now hungry to explore 'How?' How does each one of us, in our own unique circumstances, enter more fully into God's presence?

Elijah, fearing Jezebel, runs away to meet with God. God knows that His servant is exhausted emotionally as well as physically and so Elijah's first 'step' towards God is to sleep and eat. I believe in fasting and night watches as ways of focussing on God alone, yet God is supremely practical. If we want to spend more time consciously in His presence then we will need to address issues of sleep and diet – otherwise the journey will be too much for us.

Also, God honours the life stage we are in and the roles He has given us. The daily practices we adopt will depend on whether we are studying for exams, are a busy mother, in demanding work, limited by illness, or enjoying a more leisurely pace of life. Simple and 'doable' practices need to be integrated into the many things we are *already* committed to – commuting, walking the dog etc. Talking this through with one young mum we looked at programming verses onto her phone for her to meditate on whilst breastfeeding, recorded talks she could listen to while driving, noting her own love responses to her child and pondering on God's love for her, praying and praising while she walked etc. It meant taking time at the beginning of the week to stop and ask God how to prepare to meet with Him in the following days.

Elijah needed to prepare to meet with God in very practical ways – what practical steps would be helpful for *you* to take? Ask God to show you.

For prayer and reflection

Father, please guide me in my preparations to meet with You this week; highlight ways I can use my current lifestyle or adjustments I can make. Thank You. Amen.

Time in His presence (2)

Psalm 86:1–17; 1 Kings 19:9–10

'Teach me your way, O LORD, and I will walk in your truth; give me an undivided heart ...' (Psa. 86:11)

Psalm 86 is headed 'A prayer of David' and written in the context of enemy attack. It could equally be 'A prayer of Elijah'. Yesterday we looked at practical first steps in seeking God's presence. Now we ask: 'What are you doing here?'

Reasons for the things we do include: I must, I ought to, I have to, I choose to, I want to, I'd love to, I'm desperate. They range from duty and obligation to a heart response of love or fear. All are valid yet the energy varies considerably between them. Jonathan Edwards, an American pastor, wrote of the importance of 'religious affections*'. Our affections, be they love, hatred, desire, hope, fear etc, are our 'springs of action'. Without them our weak inclinations lack the necessary motivation to bring about any change in either ourselves or our situation.

Elijah's response to God's question is one that highlights fear, loneliness and despair. And God listens – repeatedly. Elijah is given the opportunity to hear his heart's cry in the presence of One who is 'forgiving and good ... abounding in love' (v.5).

Sometimes when meeting with God I sense His question, 'What is on your heart?' He doesn't ask to seek information; He already knows. He asks to help me understand all the things that are rumbling around inside me – things that need to be acknowledged if I am to meet with Him heart to heart. We come into God's presence as we are – in need of forgiveness, consolation, or ready to worship. It is the only way we can come! And it can take a while to shift our gaze from our concerns to His face and praise Him with all our heart (v.12).

*Jonathan Edwards edited by James Houston, *The Religious Affections* (Portland, Multnomah Press, 1990).

For prayer and reflection

If a friend were to ask you 'What is on your heart?' what response would you give? Take time with your answer – sometimes we need to dig below the surface issues.

WED **MAR 20**

Time in His presence (3)

1 Corinthians 3:16–18; Ephesians 4:1–7,25–32

'Don't you know that you yourselves are God's temple and that God's Spirit lives in you?' (v.16)

A friend had come to stay for a few days and I apologised that cleaning had taken a backseat for a while due to work. I also made sure that the door to my chaotic study stayed firmly shut! Why did it matter? I felt that she would enjoy her stay more if my home were clean and tidy.

When we became followers of Jesus, His Spirit took up residence in us and so every Christian already has a measure of God's presence. The measure of His presence is determined by how aligned our lives are with God and His kingdom. Hence, Jesus is described in Luke 4:1 as 'full of the Holy Spirit'. If our lives are cluttered with bitterness, rage and anger; if covered with the dust of deception; if they are dirtied by slander and malice; or if the stain of unforgiveness has not been cleansed, then the Holy Spirit is grieved. Sometimes, it's only as we seek a fuller measure of His presence that we become aware of the need for a spring clean.

I once stayed in a home where there were obvious tensions in the marriage – it was exhausting and I was glad to leave. Paul speaks of 'the unity of the Spirit' (v.3). We know that 'where two or three come together in my name, there am I with them' (Matt. 18:20). Unity with other believers matters to God, so much so that He promises to be in our midst.

If we are serious in our desire for a greater measure of God's presence in our lives we will deal with the things that grieve His Holy Spirit – our negative attitudes, words and actions towards others. Otherwise, we will end up keeping certain 'rooms' in our lives firmly closed to Him whilst giving the enemy right of access (v.27).

For prayer and reflection

The next time you do any housework or washing-up ask God to prompt you as to the things/attitudes that need to be cleaned out of your heart and mind.

Time in His presence (4)

1 Thessalonians 5:12–28

'Be joyful always; pray continually; give thanks in all circumstances, for this is God's will ...' (vv.16–18)

Over the last two years I have been trying to get fitter. It's been hard, and I am regularly tempted to give up. However, I know that, gradual though the progress may be, there is progress. Why bother? Because it affects the whole of my life.

The same is true of discipleship. It takes work; it can feel uphill; lack of obvious change is frustrating; yet surely this matters more than anything else I might do with my life. What else is this life for if not to know Him better and become like Him? Frank Laubach consciously listened to the inner voice, asking without ceasing, 'What, Father, do you desire said? What, Father, do you desire done in this minute?'* He speaks of the determination and effort required in doing this, but also of the incredible sense of cooperation with God in a plan that was far beyond himself. Is this possible for us too? Yes – many people are purchasing a phone app that alerts them to worship and pray every ten minutes, or a buzzer that does the same. When my buzzer vibrates I remind myself that I am co-labouring with Jesus and ask for His continued direction. It takes a willingness to adjust what I consider to be the priorities for the day and trust in the promptings of His Spirit.

Jesus' life was one of moment by moment obedience – always listening to the Father, always attentive to His voice, always alert to His guidance. True prayer is being 'all ears' to God and to pray continually is to tune our ears to His voice above the noise of our distractions, worries and preoccupations. Perhaps then we will know what it is to be joyful always!

*Frank Laubach, 'Letters by a Modern Mystic' quoted in *Devotional Classics* (London: Hodder & Stoughton, 1990) p.176.

For prayer and reflection

Father, please bring my attention back to You throughout today. May I hear Your voice guiding me as to what to do and say.

Time in His presence (5)

Acts 4:1–20

'... they were astonished and they took note that these men had been with Jesus.' (v.13)

'Bev, I've got to stop coming on your courses – I'm beginning to hear your voice in my head advising me on what to do in situations!' John said laughingly. He had spent 20 days on courses with me. In Jesus' time, a disciple (meaning pupil or learner) spent years with their rabbi seeking to become like him in every way – character, thinking, words, deeds and affections. Their lives were geared towards this goal: spending time in his presence, watching, listening and learning. Gradually, they became so like their rabbi that they spoke the words their rabbi spoke and did the things he did.

Peter and John had spent three years in Jesus' presence and they had been changed. The phrase 'took note' comes from a root word meaning 'known by some distinguishing mark'. So what was this mark that distinguished Peter and John? It was the presence of Jesus. They had Christ's own likeness and Spirit. Jesus said that He could 'do nothing by himself; [but] only what he sees the Father doing, because whatever the Father does the Son does also' (John 5:19). Because of this He was able to say. 'Anyone who has seen me has seen the Father' (John 14:9). Similarly, the disciples could say 'anyone who has seen me has seen Jesus.'

The goal of time in God's presence is never solely our comfort, though His ability to speak peace to the storms in our life is important. Always the hunger for His presence is the hunger of a *true* disciple – to be like Him. As we continue, next week, to look at the 'I am' sayings of Jesus, our aim will not just be to know Him better, but also to be more like Him.

For prayer and reflection

Jesus, I want to be more like You. Please help me to be a disciplined disciple, daily seeking time with You so that others may say that I 'have been with Jesus'.

WEEKEND

Time in His presence (6)

For reflection: John 12:1–19

'She poured it on Jesus' feet and wiped his feet with her hair.' *(v.3)*

We have spent this week looking at how we can more fully enter into God's presence. Psalm 100 encourages us to 'Worship the Lord with gladness; come before him with joyful songs' (v.2). John records two very different expressions of worship in today's passage: the intimate devotion of Mary and the exuberant shouts of the crowd. Whatever form worship takes for us, its importance in 'opening the gates' into God's presence cannot be overstated. Worship by its very nature is never about us – it is focusing our whole attention and gaze upon Him.

One definition I have for stress is 'forgetfulness': forgetting who we are, forgetting who God is, and forgetting that we have an enemy. Worship refreshes the memory! Henri Nouwen once had the opportunity to meet with Mother Theresa and ask her advice for his problems. She quietly said, 'Well, when you spend one hour a day adoring your Lord and never do anything which you know is wrong … you will be fine!'* Often time is like precious nard – it is costly to pour it out.

Optional further reading

Henri Nouwen, *Spiritual Direction: Wisdom for the Long Walk of Faith* (London: SPCK, 2011) p.5.

Shining lights

John 8:12–20; 1 John 1:5–10

'I am the light of the world. Whoever follows me will never walk in darkness ...' (v.12)

My friend, a lighting expert for a TV production company, advised me that I had reached that stage in life when I was better 'back-lit'. Direct light would reveal the truth that I was no longer in my thirties!

According to ancient Jewish literature there were four large menorahs (seven branched lampstands) in the Women's Courtyard of the Temple. They were about 70 feet tall. These menorahs were lit every day during the Feast of Tabernacles and were so bright that the city of Jerusalem was illuminated every night. When Jesus declared 'I am the light of the world' it is likely that He was standing by these menorahs and His listeners would have understood the power of His statement.

When we come into the presence of God we come into the light, and the truth about ourselves, our relationships and our situation is revealed. And just as the pillar of fire lit the way for the Israelites in the desert, so we find clarity and direction in God's presence – we become people who walk in the light (1 John 1:7). Walking in the light implies no passive acceptance of what the light reveals, but a willingness to deal with the sin and address the blocks to our fellowship with each other. And the truth is that sometimes we prefer the darkness, or merely to be back-lit! It is softer, easier, than choosing to change. Sometimes we don't want a 'light for our path' in case it is not the way we desire to go. Yet only by walking in the light can we, like Jesus, become the light of the world – a light shining before those around us causing them to praise our Father in heaven (Matt. 5:14–16).

For prayer and reflection

Jesus, may I bring Your light into all the situations, conversations, work and rest, that are part of my day.

Gateway to life

TUES **MAR 26**

John 10:1–10

'I am the gate; whoever enters through me will be saved.' (v.9)

Not being one who is able to sleep on transatlantic flights I was glad when we landed and I could head home to bed. Yet first there was the queue for passport control – effectively the gate into the country. Here my name and identity were checked. The computer confirmed that I was indeed a subject of Her Majesty the Queen and so had right of access to the UK.

Gates can be both means of access and barriers. So what is Jesus meaning when He states that He is 'the gate'?

In His day, it was common for shepherds to lie across the entrance to the sheepfold at night, forming a human gate stopping the sheep straying into danger and predators entering in. It involved facing the threat of thieves and wolves whose intent was to rob, kill and destroy. In the morning they would call out the names of their sheep, leading them into fresh pastures. This is the picture Jesus is painting – one of both protection and access to life in all its fullness for the sheep, and of costly sacrifice for the shepherd. And Jesus is 'the' gate – the only way into the Father's presence.

Our lives can become gates through which others access the Father or obstacles causing them to turn away from seeking Him. It is said that the first Bible non-believers 'read' is the life of the Christians whom they know. I realise that I am drawn to fellow Christians who live out their faith with integrity. They are honest about their struggles; they are unafraid of their questions, and they view life as a messy, joyful adventure guided by the Shepherd. Through the gate of their example I glimpse rich pastures and am encouraged to enter in.

For prayer and reflection

Jesus, may I never be satisfied with life in the sheepfold when You are opening a gate to new and fresh pastures. May my security be in Your protection.

Being **known**

John 10:11–30

'I am the good shepherd; I know my sheep and my sheep know me ...' (v.14)

'Open it now', was my friend's eager response as I asked whether I should await my birthday to unwrap the present she had just given me. Everything about the present indicated how well she knew me. I couldn't stop grinning! Being known is a precious thing. It takes time: time sharing our life stories, time discussing the issues we are facing; time laughing at jokes and weeping in loss. And each experience of shared time draws you imperceptibly closer.

God, who knit us together in our mother's womb, knows us intimately. Yet Jesus has said that not only are we known but also that His sheep 'know' Him. And knowing Him takes time – time in His presence, time in His Word and time walking with Him day to day listening to His voice. How well we know Him will be seen in our choices, especially when the going gets tough. If we know that it was God who led us into a situation or asked us to take on a particular role, our response will not be to head for the exit at the first sign of trouble. Instead we will wait for His voice and follow His leading.

As His sheep we know His voice. God speaks in a variety of ways – very directly through His Word, via pictures, prophetic words, sermons, unusual circumstances, the wise counsel of friends, inner promptings and even dreams. Our job is to train our ears to hear. This will involve turning down the noise that surrounds us and the preoccupations that distract, and being attentive to God's active presence. The Latin for 'obedience' includes the word 'audire' which means 'listening' – our obedience to what we have already heard tunes our ears for further listening.

For prayer and reflection

Jesus, I long to hear Your voice more clearly – please would You show me anything that deafens my ears to the things You want to say to me.

Living **our questions**

John 15:1–17

'This is to my Father's glory, that you bear much fruit, showing yourselves to be my disciples.'(v.8)

Most of us live out our questions whether or not we have articulated them to ourselves or others. For example, if on waking, the question that fills one's mind is, 'How can I get everything on my "To Do" list done?' then every phone call or chance meeting feels like an interruption. On the way home from a training course, a major road accident meant that we crawled along, adding two hours to my journey time. In the middle of this God challenged my internal question – instead of 'How long is this going to take?' He suggested 'What sort of driver do I want to be in this situation?' Effectively He changed my focus from my timetable to consideration for those around me.

One of the implications of Jesus stating 'I am the vine; you are the branches' (v.5) is that all our questions are re-ordered. Because we can do nothing fruitful and lasting without Him, our question might become, 'How do I remain in his love?' Obedience to His commands is vital to 'remaining', and remaining results in our joy being full (v.11). To obey, we need to know the words He has already spoken (v.3) and the specific direction for each day. Hence the question develops into: 'How can I be more conscious of your voice moment by moment as I seek to remain?' Remaining as part of the vine is not a problem to be solved but a journey to be taken with Jesus as our Friend and Guide. Becoming conscious of our questions and allowing the Holy Spirit to reframe them can help us on that journey.

Perhaps, like Job, our questions will one day fall away as we realise that we had spoken of things we didn't understand (Job 42:3–4).

For prayer and reflection

Think back over the last week – what questions have you been 'living'? Try to articulate your deeper questions, and don't be afraid of living without ready answers.

FRI **MAR 29**

Bread from heaven

John 6:25–42

'Then Jesus declared, "I am the bread of life. He who comes to me will never go hungry ..."' (v.35)

The book I was reading contrasted our two hungers – the greater hunger and the lesser. The author argued that the lesser hunger could be satisfied by consuming more of the world's 'stuff' – more food, clothing, bigger houses etc, whereas the greater hunger could not. This hunger was for meaning, significance and purpose in life.

At the beginning of John 6 Jesus has provided bread to satisfy the important, but lesser, hunger for food. Now He is declaring that only the bread from heaven can satisfy our greater hunger – bread that is provided directly from God as was the manna in the wilderness. And He is that bread, the Word made flesh, the bread that will satisfy and give life. So how do we 'eat' this bread?

Jesus is the bread 'broken for us'. We eat by looking to the Son and believing in Him (v.40) as the perfect sacrifice that reconciles us to God. We demonstrate our belief in Him through the way we seek to address the hunger in our lives. Too often we try to satisfy the greater hunger with the same things that satisfy the lesser hunger – more 'stuff'. If our solution to the problems and difficulties of this life is no different from that of our unbelieving neighbours then we cannot say that we do 'not live by bread alone, but on every word that comes from the mouth of God' (Matt. 4:4). True belief will result in a deep trust in our Father; the unbelief of both the Israelites in the desert and the Jews listening to Jesus was evidenced by grumbling. Might our level of dissatisfaction with the things we face each day be an indication of our need to eat again of the bread from heaven?

For prayer and reflection

Jesus, 'when I survey the wondrous cross'* on which Your body was broken for me and Your blood was shed, I kneel in thankfulness.

*'When I Survey the Wondrous Cross', Isaac Watts, 1707.

WEEKEND

Resurrection life

For reflection: John 11:17–27; Mark 15:33–41

'I am the resurrection and the life. He who believes in me will live, even though he dies.' (v.25)

He is risen! This weekend, we celebrate that death has been defeated because Jesus is the resurrection and the life. We celebrate that the sacrifice necessary for us to approach our holy God has been made and that 'the curtain of the temple was torn in two from top to bottom' (v.38) and the way into the Holy of Holies has been opened for us. We celebrate that the intimacy of His presence, enjoyed by Adam and Eve in the Garden, is now possible for us. So 'let us draw near to God with a sincere heart in full assurance of faith' (Heb. 10:22).

Together we have journeyed through the Bible, seeking both to grow our hunger to see God's face and to learn how to more fully enter into His presence. We know that to look at Jesus is to see the face of God. The head, which in sacrificial love wore a crown of thorns for us, now wears a crown of gold. As we come into His presence and worship Jesus, the King of kings, we are changed. One day 'when he appears, we shall be like him, for we shall see him as he is' (1 John 3:2). Amen!

Optional further reading

Read through one or more of the resurrection accounts in the Gospels (Matt. 28:1–15; Mark 16; Luke 24:1–49; John 20–21), reflecting on what it means for Jesus to be the resurrection and the life.

CWR TODAY

Inspiring Women Every Day on CD

For the very first time, CWR is delighted to offer readers of *Inspiring Women Every Day* a selection of meditations and Bible readings taken from the well-loved notes on audio CD. The first titles in this exciting new series, these CDs blend inspirational words and music, making them ideal for everyday use.

My Times, God's Timing

Explore the mystery of times and seasons with Carol Herzig and learn from biblical characters how to co-operate with God's unexpected timing and to invest in His eternal purposes in our lives.
EAN: 5027957001435
£9.99 incl VAT

Psalm 139

In a series of honest and engaging reflections, meditate with Chris Ledger on the key truths of this much-loved psalm and recognise that God delights in each one of us as His masterpiece.
EAN: 5027957001442
£9.99 incl VAT

Inspired by Inspiring *Women Every Day*.
Previous readers have been greatly helped by these notes:

'I was really encouraged and rejuvenated as a woman and as a child of God by the notes on "My Times, God's Timing". They gave me courage to always take my position in the Lord and an understanding in going through different seasons in the Christian walk.' Constance

'I loved the notes "My Times, God's Timing". Very thought and prayer provoking ... I was particularly inspired by the day entitled "A time for everything" which helped me to hear from the Lord and focus on my family and others around me who do not know Him and are in great need.' Lea

Visit **www.cwr.org.uk/store** or a Christian bookshop, to obtain your copy.

The Big Story – Genesis to Revelation

Led by Philip Greenslade

Join us on this exciting course and explore with gifted Bible teacher Philip Greenslade the narrative of Scripture to gain understanding of the deep underlying structure of the Bible and the overarching redemptive strategy of God. This includes, how the important pieces of the Bible narrative fit together and how our personal stories relate to God's bigger story.

Venue: Waverley Abbey House

Tues–Sat 28 May – 1 June

£450 Residential/£350 Non-residential

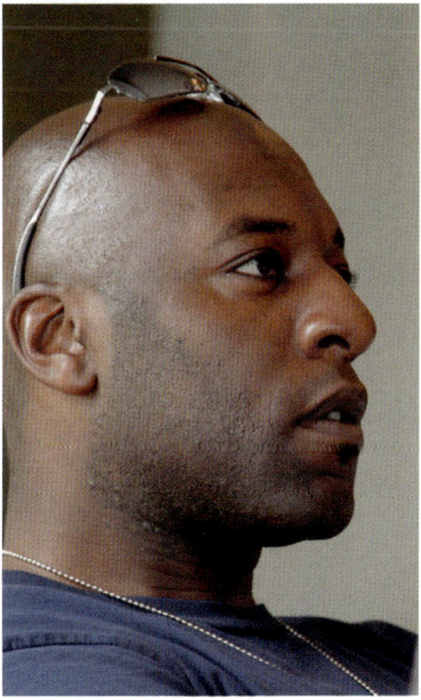

God's Questions

Led by Philip Greenslade

For more information and to book places, visit www.cwr.org.uk/training or call +44 (0)1252 784719

Venue: Waverley Abbey House

Mon–Wed 23–25 September

£235 Residential/£180 Non-residential

Early Bird Prices £211.50 Residential/ £162 Non-residential (up to 1 July 2013)

Future Bible Discovery Weekend

Venue: Waverley Abbey House

Fri–Sun 8–10 November

'A wonderful experience; clear, challenging, helpful and inspiring teacing; great company, food and rest.'

Pastoral Care in the Local Church

Led by Stuart Pascall, Lynn Penson and the CWR Tutor Team

Lives and communities are transformed as people feel cared for. Come with us and explore God's passionate heart for caring, God's affirming call, God's equipping grace and God's effective people. Whether leading or being involved in a pastoral care team, or just exploring your pastoral gifting, this course will enlarge your vision of the Church's calling to pastoral care. It will help you develop your caring skills, whether using them individually or as part of a wider team.

Venue: Waverley Abbey House

Mon–Fri 11–15 March

£450 Residential/£350 Non-residential

'This course is to be highly recommended; inspirational practical teaching in a beautiful, relaxed and friendly environment.'

Introduction to Biblical Care and Counselling

Led by Angie Coombes, Richard Laws and team

This five-day foundation course is an ideal way to begin learning how to put your desire to help people into effective practice. You will be encouraged to reflect on your own life in the light of the biblical model presented, before using the principles to help others. Our approach has transformed the lives of so many who have been on this course. Key features include: the biblical basis for pastoral care and counselling, how to deal with life's basic issues successfully and essential facts every people-helper should know.

Venue: Waverley Abbey House

Mon–Fri 18–22 March, Mon–Fri 12–16 August, Mon–Fri 18–22 November

Venue: Pilgrim Hall

Mon–Fri 10–14 June

£450 Residential/£350 Non-residential

For further info/To book: **www.cwr.org.uk** or call **+44 (0)1252 784719**.
Prices and dates correct at the time of printing.

WAVERLEY RESIDENTIAL COURSES AND EVENTS 2013

Bible Discovery: The Pebble who Became a Rock

Led By Philip Greenslade

Tracking Peter's faith journey from big fisherman to founding apostle, as recorded in the Gospels, Acts and 1 and 2 Peter, we will be led to revalue the man described by New Testament scholar Martin Hengel as 'the underestimated apostle', and we will be encouraged and challenged by his amazing story.

Venue: Pilgrim Hall

Tues–Thurs 7–9 May

£215 Residential/£162 Non-residential

Bible Discovery Weekend – Famous Last Words

Led by Philip Greenslade

Often acknowledged as the apostle Paul's 'last word' and final testimony, his Second Letter to Timothy is also perhaps his most personal epistle. He writes from a pastoral heart with tough love to instruct, inspire and invigorate the young pastor, Timothy, who has been his 'son' in the faith. 'Every part of Scripture is God-breathed and useful one way or another – showing us truth, exposing our rebellion, correcting our mistakes, training us to live God's way.'

Venue: Waverley Abbey House

Fri–Sun 21–23 June

£215 Residential/£162 Non-residential

Early Bird Prices £193.50 Residential/£145.80 Non-residential (Up to 29 March 2013)

For further info/To book: **www.cwr.org.uk** or call **+44 (0)1252 784719**.
Prices and dates correct at the time of printing.

Women's Weekend - In the Palm of His Hand

Led by Lynn Penson and Beverley Shepherd

What part of the body do we use to welcome, to give, to restrain, to love, to create, to bring healing, to guide, to help? Our hands. Scripture uses wonderful pictures of God's hands as doing all this and much more beside. During this week we will be exploring what it means to be held secure in, and sustained by, the loving hands of God and how we can become 'God's hands' to others. This is a wonderful opportunity for you to draw closer to God and be renewed. You will enjoy meeting new friends and the good food too!

Venue: Pilgrim Hall

Fri-Sun 5-7 July

£185 Residential/£135 Non-residential

Early Bird Prices £166.50 Residential/£121.50 Non-residential (Up to 12 April 2013)

Woman to Woman

Led by Lynn Penson and team

This unique course is designed for women of all ages who want to help and minister to other women, whether on a one-to-one basis, leading a small group or with responsibility for a church or area-wide group. The course is brimming with opportunities to learn and grow as you understand more about yourself and explore your gifts, vision, spirituality and abilities. The weekend includes: establishing biblical foundations, developing visions and goals, identifying your spiritual gifting and much more.

Venue: Pilgrim Hall

Mon-Fri 17-21 June

£450 Residential/£350 Non-residential

Early Bird Prices £405 Residential/£315 Non-residential (Up to 25 March 2013)

'It has been helpful in my own personal walk with the Lord, and has provided a toolbox with which to go and help others.'

OTHER WOMEN'S WEEKENDS IN 2013

Pilgrim Hall:

Fri-Sun 25-27 October

£185 Residential/£135 Non-residential

Early Bird Prices £166.50 Residential/£121.50 Non-residential (Up to 2 August 2013)

Waverley Abbey House:

Fri-Sun 29 November - 1 December

£185 Residential/£135 Non-residential

Early Bird Prices £166.50 Residential/£121.50 Non-residential (Up to 6 September 2013)

Certificate in Counselling Supervision - Stages 1 and 2

Led by Heather Churchill

The overall aim of the course is to equip delegates with the necessary skills and knowledge to provide supervisory support and guidance to counsellors in clinical practice. The course will assist delegates to:

- Understand the purpose and role of supervision
- Consider ethical and legal responsibilities of supervision, including boundaries and contract issues
- Understand the theories and models of supervising both individuals and groups
- Develop the necessary skills to establish an effective working alliance
- Evaluate the supervisory process, including their own practice of supervision
- Understand life cycles of groups and group dynamics in group supervision

Venue: Waverley Abbey House

Stage 1: Mon–Tues 4–5 March

Stage 2: Mon–Tues 20–21 May

£475 Residential/£420 Non-residential (Includes both Stage 1 and Stage 2)

Preparation for Marriage

Led by Mick & Lynette Brooks with Lynn & Andrew Penson

Build a firm biblical foundation as you consider the nature of Christian marriage, love and sexuality. With help from the Myers-Briggs Type Indicator®, develop mutual understanding and learn to handle conflict and avoid marriage breakdown, as you identify the strengths, weaknesses and potential stress points in your relationship.

Venue: Waverley Abbey House

Fri–Sun 1–3 March

£410 Residential per couple

(£205 per person if being paid for separately)

Marriage on Track

Led by Lynn & Andrew Penson

Enjoy a weekend together in beautiful surroundings offering the opportunity to consider what Christian marriage means and explore topics such as communication, handling conflict, sexual intimacy, expressing love and understanding your partner with the help of the Myers-Briggs Type Indicator®. Celebrate your marriage with a romantic dinner *a deux* on Saturday evening!

Venue: Waverley Abbey House

Fri–Sun 11–13 October

£410 Residential per couple

Early Bird Price £369 (up to 19 July 2013)

For further info/To book: **www.cwr.org.uk** or call **+44 (0)1252 784719**.
Prices and dates correct at the time of printing.

WOMEN'S WEEKENDS

Women's weekends offer time and space to enjoy the company of God and others, to listen, laugh and share, to reflect creatively and pray in the beautiful surroundings.

Springs of Life

Led by Nicky-Sue Terry and Ros Derges

What we hold in our hearts affects the way we experience life, and Jesus wants us to enjoy an abundant life. What are our hearts like? What is it that we are to guard? We can pray with the psalmist, 'Search me, O God, and know my heart' (Psalm 139:23). Jesus knew people's hearts, and His teaching inspires us to develop hearts that are pure, generous, forgiving and loving. Like His, our hearts are to reflect something of God's heart. Join us as we explore the richness of life that our hearts can hold and impart, as we seek to become women after God's own heart.

Venue: Waverley Abbey House

Fri–Sun 26–28 April

£185 Residential/£135 Non-residential

God's Positioning System

Ecclesiastes 1:1–2; Isaiah 40:1–8

'"Meaningless! Meaningless!" says the Teacher. "Utterly meaningless! Everything is meaningless."' (Eccl. 1:2)

Your heart might have sunk when you picked up this month's Bible-reading notes. 'Ecclesiastes? Isn't that just a book about misery?' I bet with the year well under way and all its accompanying stresses you were hoping for a bit of a pick-me-up. And I can't blame you. But let me encourage you that despite its depressing opening verses and periodic meanderings into despair, this beautiful book is full of hope and faith – just perfect to meditate upon having been reminded of God's central purposes on Easter Sunday.

Many Bible scholars believe that it was written by King Solomon towards the end of his reign in the years leading up to 930 BC.* The author identifies himself as 'the Teacher', a son of David, king of Jerusalem, and we will be looking in more detail at the life of Solomon in our weekend readings.

The key to understanding this book is the phrase 'under the sun' (1:9). You will notice that the diatribes against meaninglessness and folly are always followed by it and speak of life on earth without God. In contrast, when the author writes of godly wisdom (7:11) and gifts from God (5:19), he is advocating a life full of meaning.

Like you and I, the author's life is a mix of periods of meaning and meaninglessness. There are times when everything makes sense and others when we don't have a clue where we are or what's going on. Ecclesiastes gives us a bird's eye view of life in all its confusion. But one thing is clear: only God can help us make sense of it all. He is like a GPS – a global positioning system, or, as I like to think of it, God's Positioning System.

*For further details see: Michael Eaton, *Ecclesiastes: An Introduction and Commentary (Tyndale Old Testament Commentary*, (Leicester: Inter Varsity Press, 1983).

For prayer and reflection

Father, I thank You that though my life is at times confusing, You are always with me. Help me to trust that even though I don't always know where I'm going, You do. Amen.

TUES **APR 2**

Life's **merry-go-round**

Ecclesiastes 1:1–11; Matthew 28:20b

'What has been will be again, what has been done will be done again; there is nothing new under the sun.' (Eccl. 1:9)

I have been keeping a spiritual journal since my late teens. It started simply as a tool to help me keep track of my prayer times: who and what to pray for, and a check-list of my sins. But over the years it has become so much more. It is a record of my communication with God; it is my personal book of psalms; it declares in scrawling ink the highs and lows, the confusion and clarity of my soul's journey with God.

It also reminds me of God's words to me: 'I will always be with you.' He impressed that upon my heart through Matthew 28:20, the day I first decided to walk with Him. I was 11 years old. Now, 31 years later, my journal is tangible evidence that He has kept His promise. I sometimes re-read parts to see the fingerprints of God on my life. And like the author of Ecclesiastes, I see that there is nothing new under the sun. Life is like a merry-go-round and it feels at times like I'm chasing after the wind.

Many of my struggles are the same as they were 10 or 15 years ago. The other day I was reading my journal for 1998. It was a time of transition, as I was leaving full-time Christian work to get a job in the secular world. I was confused and uncertain; I thought God was leading me, but sometimes I wasn't sure. 'Don't worry,' I said to my past self with the benefit of 14 years of hindsight, 'you'll get through this.' Now once again I'm in a time of transition. My husband has just been made redundant and my job isn't secure. But I'm sure in ten years I'll look back on this journal and say: 'Don't worry; God will bring you through.'

For prayer and reflection

Have you ever kept a spiritual journal? Why not start one today. Just write down your thoughts and prayers and what you think God is saying to you now.

'It's **education**, stupid'

Ecclesiastes 1:12–18; Luke 2:41–52

'I devoted myself to study and to explore by wisdom all that is done under heaven.' (Eccl. 1:13)

A few years ago I was asked by two different universities to lecture in scriptwriting and journalism. With my Masters' degree, I am probably well-educated by most people's standards, but on entering these institutions I started to feel pretty dumb. Although the jobs did not require academic qualifications but practical experience in the media industry, coincidentally, the job offers had come at a time when I had just started a part-time PhD.

For the next 18 months I tried to juggle my new workload and my studies along with being a mother and wife. I was at breaking point. I had to give up one of them but was loathe to let the PhD go. I was enjoying my studies and like Solomon, relished '[exploring] by wisdom' all there was to know in my field. I had also by then applied for a more fixed contract but was turned down because I did not yet have a PhD.

So what was my real motivation? I think part of it might have been to prove that I was just as 'clever' as my colleagues; but by thinking that I was shown to be a fool. Education is no mark of wisdom. Jesus probably had a very limited education compared to the great scholars of His time; but even as a boy He confounded them with His understanding. And as Solomon was to discover: 'With much wisdom comes much sorrow; the more knowledge, the more grief' (Eccl. 1:18).

Education may help grease the wheels to get a better job (although even that is not guaranteed these days) but it will not make you any wiser than anyone else. Wisdom comes from the heart, not the head.

For prayer and reflection

Father, thank You that true wisdom comes from You and that no amount of study can replace the knowledge You place in our hearts. Amen.

THURS **APR 4**

The **makeover show**

Ecclesiastes 2:1–11

'I undertook great projects: I built houses for myself and planted vineyards.' (v.4)

Have you ever watched a TV makeover show?

Step 1: we are introduced to a person or family who are dissatisfied with the way their life is. Either their physical appearance, wardrobe or home environment does not reflect who they feel they really are on the inside but they don't know how, or can't afford, to change it.

Step 2: we are introduced to the makeover team. In under ten minutes they analyse what's wrong with the person or their environment and introduce their improvement plan.

Step 3: the client resists/argues/compromises/cries – but finally capitulates.

Step 4: the house/garden/wardrobe/person is completely stripped.

Step 5: the will of the makeover team is imposed on the blank canvas.

Step 6: the client is over-awed with the new life that has been created and swears that they will keep it this way.

Step 7: well, that's the bit we don't see ...

I secretly yearn for a makeover team to rush into my life and make me over in an hour, day or at most a week. I can never achieve the 'look' myself because I've got to use the stuff I've already got. And my daughter's toys and my husband's gadgets and my books and the dogs' beds all need to fit in somewhere.

But thank God they do, because those things and the people they belong to are what make our house our home. I think God feels the same way. His re-make of our lives is rarely an overnight gutting and revamp; rather He works with what we've already got and slowly brings order out of chaos.

For prayer and reflection

Father, I confess that I dream of being made-over like they do on TV. Forgive me for not appreciating what I've already got. Lord, make me over from the inside out. Amen.

The Wind in the Willows

Ecclesiastes 2:12–16; Matthew 14:22–36

'The wise man has eyes in his head, while the fool walks in the darkness; but I came to realise that the same fate overtakes them both.' (Eccl. 2:14)

In *The Wind in the Willows* by Kenneth Grahame, we are introduced to the residents of the Riverside whom Mole meets on his adventures to explore life beyond his hole. His two best friends are Ratty and Toad. Ratty is extremely sensible and cautious and Toad extremely spontaneous; but as his reckless lifestyle leads him into ever-deepening trouble, he proves to be extremely foolish too.

After getting sent to prison for 20 years for stealing and crashing a car, Toad escapes only to discover that his beloved home, Toad Hall, has been overtaken by stoats and weasels. Toad is repentant and asks his friends to help him reclaim his property. But the judgmental Ratty only concedes to help when Toad reluctantly agrees never to do anything foolish or reckless again. The friends defeat the dastardly interlopers and have a party to celebrate. But Toad is not allowed to give one of his famous speeches or do anything extravagant. He's miserable. Eventually, Mole persuades Ratty to let Toad be Toad. The book ends with the reader feeling that both Toad and Ratty have compromised and grown; one has become slightly more cautious and the other a tad more adventurous.

In the New Testament, Peter is a bit like Mr Toad. Although his recklessness sometimes got him into trouble, his adventurous nature enabled him to take risks – like walking on water!

In today's passage Solomon writes of wisdom and foolishness and realises that neither is the answer. Only a life guided by God can bring the balance that is needed between the two. Are you a Ratty or a Toad?

For prayer and reflection

Dear Lord, help me to be more adventurous when I need to step out in faith and more cautious when I need to wait on Your will. Amen.

WEEKEND

The Life of Solomon – a fresh start

For reflection: 2 Samuel 12:11–25

'Bathsheba ... gave birth to a son, and they named him Solomon. The LORD loved him ...' (12:24)

Solomon is believed to have written Ecclesiastes. He was the son of the adulterous King David and Bathsheba. David had lusted after Bathsheba when she was already married. So he arranged to have her husband killed. Then he married Bathsheba, who may already have been pregnant. After the baby was born, the prophet Nathan confronted David with his sin. David did not try to make excuses and repented wholeheartedly. He was prepared to die, if necessary, but instead the child died and we are told this was a consequence of his sin. David 'comforted' Bathsheba and she became pregnant again. I should imagine they feared this second child would also be taken from them. But he wasn't. God had forgiven them and the past was in the past. Solomon was born and we are told that 'The LORD loved him ...'

Do you fear the consequences of your past sin will return? Have you suffered loss and expect the same thing to happen again? Allow the past to remain in the past. Trust that God loves you now. You too can have a fresh start.

Optional further reading

Read the full story in 2 Samuel 11–12; Michael Eaton, *Ecclesiastes: An Introduction and Commentary (Tyndale Old Testament Commentary)* (Leicester: Inter Varsity Press, 1983).

The **daily grind**

Ecclesiastes 2:17–26; Colossians 3:22–4:1

'So my heart began to despair over all my toilsome labour under the sun.' (Eccl. 2:20)

I have a love/hate relationship with work. On the positive side it fulfils me socially, creatively and intellectually as well as providing some money. But there are other aspects (like the never-ending pile of marking!) that drain me. Added to this are the inevitable workplace conflicts, trying to fit all my family commitments and housework in, and the resentment when my pay rarely reflects the actual time I've spent doing the work.

But I'm also aware that I am blessed to have a job. Many people have been laid-off or are struggling to find their first job since leaving full-time education, or have retired but miss their work. Then I consider women in other parts of the world who have never had the opportunity to work out of the home – not by choice but by oppression. At times like this I have to take myself in hand.

Solomon also moaned about his work. (Although as a rich man in a patriarchal, slave-owning culture, I doubt he had to worry about scrubbing floors and cleaning toilets between all his kingly activities!) But let's forgive him that and consider that being a ruler of a nation can be a difficult job.

So what's the answer? Paul suggests in Colossians that whatever work we do we need to do it as a service to God, not man. So how does that work out in practice? As an experiment over the next few weeks I'm going to pray for every one of my 120 students whilst I mark their assignments. That way my most hated task will become an act of worship. At least that's the plan.

For prayer and reflection

What is your attitude towards your daily work (whether in the home or out of it)? What practical steps can you take to make your working experience an act of worship?

TUES **APR 9**

God's seasons

Ecclesiastes 3:1–8

'There is a time for everything, and a season for every activity under heaven.' (v.1)

I am writing this in a rented country cottage. There are lambs in the fields. There are blue tits and robins building their nests and a male pheasant impressing his mate. Spring flowers are everywhere; the world is full of hope. The last time I was here was 18 months ago. It was the end of autumn and birds were fewer. A fox wandered by but didn't stop, hurrying home before the winter snow set in. Nature has its seasons. There is a time to be born and a time to die; a time to plant and a time to uproot.

We also have patterns in our lives: we are born, we grow up; we die. In between we may get married and have children; we learn; we work; we retire. Spiritually too there are seasons. There is a period of awakening to the whispers of the Holy Spirit; then the moment of immense relief when we ask God to inhabit our hearts. There is the season of rapid growth as we devour the Word and enter into discipleship. There is excitement when we glimpse a potential future and the lull of disappointment when we never seem to reach it. There are the dark nights when God cannot be felt, the spring mornings when hope is renewed, the summery days when we are comfortable in His companionship and the autumn-like years as we grow older and prepare to meet Him face to face.

Recognising your spiritual season allows you to have grace for your soul. Do not be frustrated if you are no longer busy doing things for God when He has called you to a time of preparation or withdrawal. But learn too to recognise when He is stirring you again to enter a new season of growth.

For prayer and reflection

Father, help me to recognise the spiritual season of my life and grace to embrace all You have for me within it. Amen.

The Ghost of **Christmas Past**

Ecclesiastes 3:9–15

'Whatever is has already been, and what will be has been before; and God will call the past to account.' (v.15)

Last Christmas we introduced our daughter to Monopoly. My husband was keen to buy it, but I was reluctant. I wasn't really sure why I didn't want to get the game other than I hadn't enjoyed it as a child. It was only when we started playing that I remembered why. One of my family members had been a shameless cheat and used to steal money from the bank, claim he owned property when he didn't and refuse to pay when rent was demanded from him. It always ended up in a big argument. When my dad was asked to intervene he never did to my satisfaction. He declared it was 'only a game' and we should get over it. But I wanted the great injustice to be dealt with and for it to be recognised that I was the victim of someone else's 'sin'.

On reflection I see how that feeling of injustice has carried through into other areas of my life. But more of that in tomorrow's reflection. For today I want to tell you about how I realised last Christmas that I needed to forgive that family member for his 'sins' against me – and yes, there was more to it all than Monopoly. When the Ghost of Christmas Past comes we can stew over the memories and wallow in our pain or we can ask God to help us face it. Getting back to Monopoly: I could have refused to play because it made me angry remembering how it used to be. But then I would have missed the joy of seeing my daughter learn a new skill and share the fun of family time. So I chose to let go of the past. Oh, and she won fair and square: no cheating involved.

For prayer and reflection

What happens when the Ghost of Christmas Past comes to visit you? Take those memories to God now and ask Him to heal you and help you forgive.

THURS **APR 11**

When life's **not fair**

Ecclesiastes 3:16–22; Revelation 21:1–5

'In the place of judgment – wickedness was there. In the place of justice – wickedness was there.' (Eccl. 3:16)

I became aware of injustice in the world from an early age. As I've grown older this has broadened from the Monopoly board to the countries of the world. When my daughter asks why we send a Christmas parcel to a child in Tanzania I say that it's because they don't have money. 'But why doesn't Santa take presents to them too?' she asks. Good question. However, whether the gifts come from Santa, God or relief agencies the fact remains: they are not evenly distributed. Neither are famine, tsunamis and war. Granted, some First World countries suffer natural disasters, but they have the resources to limit the damage. They also have the infrastructure to save their children from treatable diseases that elsewhere snuff out a third of under 5s every year.

Before the Christian era and introduction of the idea that God loves everyone equally, people did not worry about such things. Gods were capricious and loved some people more than others or did not love at all; fairness was not expected. So what are we to do when the evidence suggests God's love is not shared out equally? Jesus could have come and changed the world in one go. But He didn't. For some reason He wanted us to be the vehicle of that change. Like a stone dropped in a puddle, God's goodness ripples out to change the world around it. I may not be able to affect the whole world, but perhaps I might have an impact in my own little puddle. And if I flick to Revelation at the end of the Bible I'm reminded of God's promise that one day His love will cover the whole earth and wickedness will no longer flourish in the place of justice.

For prayer and reflection

Lord, I don't know why You allow injustice to flourish when You could stop it. But I do know You love all people equally. Help me to be a vehicle of that love. Amen.

The importance of **friends**

Ecclesiastes 4:1–12; John 19:25–27

'If one falls down, his friend can help him up. But pity the man who falls and has no one to help him up!' (Eccl. 4:10)

Solomon was born into a large family full of rivalries and factions. Unlike his father David, it does not seem that Solomon had anyone close to him, despite being surrounded by people. This passage suggests a yearning for companionship.

Friends are important. But they need to be cultivated or they can easily be lost. Sometimes this is through a falling out, but more often it's simply through drifting apart. Friendship is a two-way street. I am saddened by once-good friends who have stopped corresponding with me and I'm sure I have disappointed other people by my lack of effort too. My single friends are much better at friendship than I am. They realise the need to invest in those relationships. When you are married, family can easily become your focus to the exclusion of your friends. But a balance needs to be maintained.

Jesus appeared to be closer to His friends than His family and asked His friend John to look after His mother when He died. Why did He do this when the Bible tells us He had a number of real brothers who could do the job? Jesus knew that blood relationships were not by definition stronger than friendships. We can't choose our family but we can choose our friends. Love by choice is stronger than love by duty. Friendship has been designed by God to fill our need to be loved and supported. In the Bible we hear of a number of different words for love – one of them is *philia*, which is the love of a friend. Too often we think that romantic attachments are the only way to fill our need to be loved. But that's not how God has created us. We need friends too.

For prayer and reflection

Think about a friendship that is in danger of fading. Spend some time now praying about it. Then take some action to rekindle it.

WEEKEND

The Life of Solomon – the gift of wisdom

For reflection: 1 Kings 3:1–15

'... give your servant a discerning heart ... to distinguish between right and wrong.' (v.9)

When Solomon succeeded his father as king, God offered to give him a coronation present. Solomon could have asked for anything and, we assume, God would have given it to him. But although he was young (Solomon refers to himself as a 'little child'; he was probably around 20 years old when he was offered the throne) he was not filled with the typical youthful conviction that he could do anything. Solomon realised that to bring together a kingdom in danger of being torn apart by rival factions, he needed supernatural support. He had brothers who were closer in the line of succession; and one of them, Adonijah, had already declared himself king. There were still a number of unresolved tensions from David's reign within the family and the kingdom itself. David, the warrior king and poet, was a hard act to follow. Solomon knew he needed help and was humble enough to ask for it. Solomon, the boy king, soon consolidated his position – not through force of arms but a wisdom that became the renown of the ancient world.

Optional further reading

The early reign of King Solomon: 1 Kings 1–4; a snapshot of his wisdom: Proverbs 21–23.

SPECIAL ARTICLE

A Spiritual Spring Clean

The following extract by **Lynn Penson** is taken from *Seasons – Embracing the Rhythms of Life*, published by CWR in 2011.

So how can we be getting ready for our spiritual summer whilst also enjoying the present spring? As I look back on the various new paths I have taken I am reminded of the ways I have prepared for what is to come.

Find suitable training

Following my most recent extended 'winter experiences' I knew it was time to move onwards and decided that my next move was to apply for the Certificate in Christian Counselling at Waverley. This equipped me wonderfully for the plans God had for me. For you, it may be a day, evening, weekend, week-long or even longer course that will equip you better. Maybe it is learning to drive, attending a creative writing course or art class, or preparing for active service in retirement. Or it may be about getting ready for marriage or childbirth with marriage preparation or parenting classes to consider.

Read

Scour your local library, bookshops, friends' and minister's bookshelves for relevant books and magazine articles.

Talk to people who know you

Listen to advice from wise people who can see your gifts and potential. If you feel a calling to some activity within your church discuss it with your church leaders so that you remain within the authority structure of the church.

Spend time with people who are faith-builders and avoid people who will be discouraging

It is good to get advice from people who are realistic and can spot difficulties for you, but if something inside you has ignited a passion, take care to nurture it by being in the company of those who can share and encourage your vision.

Research and explore
When I first felt drawn to leading women's conferences in my area of Dorset I got as much information as possible; finding out what was already available, what other churches were doing, and how other people advertised.

Spend time with God
Although last on this list, it needs to be central to any plan of action for all seasons, not just for spring. It may be setting aside time to go on retreat, or just retreating with God while at home. Walking, driving, swimming or other activities where you are able to quieten your voice in order to hear His voice can be useful times when used intentionally. Remember that *listening to* God is more effective than *talking at* Him. You may hear God through everyday circumstances; by reading books, through music, in a sermon, through the comments and advice of people you trust, through creation and so many other ways.

One important way of hearing from God is by reading His Word – the Bible. As we read Scripture so God can speak through it to our situations.

Your word is a lamp to my feet and a light for my path.

Psalm 119:105

When the writers of the psalms were referring to the word or words of God, they were not thinking of the Bible. The Old Testament did not exist as such and the New Testament accounts had yet to happen. However, Christians since the Early Church have believed that the Bible, although written by many individuals, contains God's words to us. And so we are in agreement with the psalmist when he writes, 'Your word is a light for my path', when we acknowledge that we can discover ways in which God is guiding us through reading Scripture, and allowing His principles and priorities to take central place in our lives.

Hearing through Scripture

It is good to vary the way we read the Bible. Sometimes reading a complete book in one sitting, for example a New Testament letter, can be helpful. Other times it is better to concentrate on smaller segments, or even a phrase or word. When it comes to biblical meditation, I like the picture of a cow chewing the cud. The cow gets all the goodness out of the food which then goes into its stomach. However, that is not the end of it as the semi-digested food, the cud, returns from the stomach to the mouth to be chewed a second and third time. This way the cow can extract the very best out of every mouthful.

Just as the idiomatic expression 'chewing the cud' means meditating or pondering, over a prolonged period, to meditate on a passage of Scripture requires time to read and reread, to get as much out of it as possible and then to go back for more!

Seasons –
Embracing the Rhythms of Life
by Lynn Penson
ISBN: 978-1-85345-605-3

Available direct from CWR **+44 (0)1252 784710**, online at **www.cwr.org.uk/store** or from Christian bookshops.

Seminars for your church

CWR has a wide range of popular seminars specifically designed for women that we would be delighted to bring to your church. These include: Being a Secure Woman, More Than You Can Handle Alone, Seasons – Embracing the Rhythms of Life and Designed for Living. These seminars are taught by tutors who are part of the CWR Ministry to Women Team and, if desired, can be adapted to full or half-day seminars.

For further information visit **www.cwr.org.uk/regional**
Call: **01252 784719** Email: **training@cwr.org.uk**

MON **APR 15**

Wisdom and age

Ecclesiastes 4:13–16; Ephesians 6:1–4

'Better a poor but wise youth than an old but foolish king who no longer knows how to take warning.' (Eccl. 4:13)

It is said that wisdom comes with age, but this is not always the case. I am now in my early forties; what is called 'middle-aged'. Am I any wiser than I was at twenty? In many ways, yes; I have seen and experienced a lot in twenty-odd years. But I am only wiser in the areas where I have learnt from my mistakes and grown in character. There are many things I have lost in the last two decades: a desire to give everything up and go wherever God calls me; a passion to sacrifice my own comfort for the sake of fighting for justice; is that growing into wisdom? What we sometimes refer to as wisdom may simply be cynicism or plain laziness. The other day my husband said that when he was in his teens and early twenties he would look at people in their forties in the church and wonder why they weren't 'doing more for God'. 'And now you realise it's just because they were too tired!' I said, and we both laughed.

When I was 18 I went with my dad to apply for a university loan. The bank manager directed all his questions at my father, ignoring me completely. My dad obviously knew about his own financial affairs but he didn't know much about mine, as I was the one who had done all the research. So every time the manager asked him something, he had to ask me then pass the information back to the manager. I eventually snapped and said to the manager: 'Look, why don't you just save us all some time and ask me directly.'

'Because, my dear,' he said patronisingly, 'you are not an adult.' In today's passage Solomon realises that wisdom and age do not always grow together. Let us not look down on the young.

For prayer and reflection

Consider your attitude to people who are younger and older than you. Do you judge them or make assumptions about them just because of their age? Ask God to forgive you.

Bargaining with God

Ecclesiastes 5:1–7

'It is better not to vow than to make a vow and not fulfil it.' (v.5)

'If you let me go out to play *now* mummy, I'll tidy my room later,' is a frequently heard oath in our house. I know that my daughter will not fulfil her vow. She will come in from playing and be too tired. Then there will be dinner time, bath time and bed time. If I remind her about it she'll say: 'Tomorrow, I promise.' She can't see far enough into the future to know that when circumstances are different, she will not have the time nor inclination to fulfil the vow. But I can.

In this passage Solomon is warning his readers not to be too hasty to make deals with God. The temple messenger he refers to (v.6) would have been sent to the house of the vow-maker to remind him to pay up. In Bible times vows would have been made verbally in the Temple in the presence of a priest. They would usually have involved some kind of pledge of money ('corban' – Mark 7:11) or crops. In the case of Samuel's mother Hannah, she pledged her son to the service of the Temple (1 Sam. 1:27–28).

It seemed as if it were common practice for deals to be made with God – deals which later, when the temple messenger came to collect, would suddenly be reneged upon.

It is human nature to try to negotiate deals to our advantage. When we are faced with something bigger than ourselves – infertility, the lack of a life partner, a dream job that seems out of reach – the only person we can turn to is God. He alone is big enough to intervene and grant us our heart's desire. But I don't think God needs us to 'do a deal' with Him. If it is in His will to answer our petition, He will do so – in His time and in His way. If it isn't, He won't.

For prayer and reflection

Lord, give me the grace to accept Your yes as yes and Your no as no. Help me too to realise that I do not have to 'pay' You for Your goodness. Amen.

WED **APR 17**

The pursuit of **riches**

Ecclesiastes 5:8–6:6

'... whoever loves wealth is never satisfied with his income.' (Eccl. 5:10b)

The other day I was marking student assignments. They had done particularly well for seemingly little work and I told a friend that I was 'giving out firsts like bankers' bonuses'. We are all familiar with the fat cats at the top of society awarding themselves massive payouts for what the rest of us consider to be very little work. But do the bankers themselves think they don't deserve it? I doubt it. I remember seeing a news report where well-dressed workers in the City were asked if they thought they were paid too much. None of them said they were.

At the other end of the scale, I remember resigning from my first job because I felt I was not being paid well enough for the amount of work I was putting in. However, I doubt the woman who cleaned the toilets or the homeless man who begged at the intersection would think I wasn't getting 'enough'.

When is enough, enough? In today's passage, after outlining the unjust social scale of wealth (vv.8–9), Solomon suggests there are two sides to the money question. On the one hand there are those who 'love money' and are never satisfied with their income (v.10). He reminds them that no matter how much or little they earn they cannot take it with them when they die. On the other hand, he recognises that wealth can be a gift from God to be enjoyed (5:18–6:6) and yet some people fail to appreciate it. The key is to recognise that it's a blessing and to do good with the money you have, not to wish for more.

For prayer and reflection

God promises to meet all our needs. However, that does not always translate into material wealth. Thank God today for the blessings He has given you.

When food **doesn't fill you**

THURS **APR 18**

Ecclesiastes 6:7–12; John 4:13–15

'All man's efforts are for his mouth, yet his appetite is never satisfied.' (Eccl. 6:7)

The last thing I want to do is add to the vilification of the bigger person. In recent years our weight, and our right to choose whether or not to change it, has stopped being a private issue and has moved into the realm of public policy. With headlines screaming: 'Obesity could bankrupt the NHS', the authorities are working overtime to change the nation's waistline.

Fat is a visible vice. Issues with overeating are far more difficult to hide than drinking, smoking and participating in reckless activities, all of which have negative affects on the NHS too. Nine per cent of the health budget may be spent on the obese but between £300 and £400 million a year are 'wasted' on people with stress-related illnesses within the health sector alone.*

It's not a bad thing to encourage healthier bodies and lifestyles. Good health is a precious thing; but what concerns me in the politicisation of fat is the stigmatising of people who are considered a burden on tax-payers' pockets. And that's what it comes down to: your fat is no longer just your business because it has an impact on the girth of *my* wallet.

So I would like to broaden today's discussion to discuss appetite in the sense of consumption. Yesterday we spoke about financial consumption and the need to always have more. Think about whatever you consume, greedily. For some of you that may well be food. Now ask yourself what you are trying to fill. As today's readings both show, our physical appetites mask something deeper. What we really need to fill us is God. If you 'eat' out of boredom, or sadness or stress you will never truly be filled.

*Source: 'Workplace Stress', NHS Employers, 2007.

For prayer and reflection

Lord, help me today to replace my appetite for the things that are not good for me with an appetite for You. Fill me to overflowing, Lord. Amen.

FRI **APR 19**

The limits of **human wisdom**

Ecclesiastes 7:15–25; Matthew 14:25–31

'"I am determined to be wise" – but this was beyond me.' (Eccl. 7:23)

I once heard about a young missionary trainee who decided to put his faith to the test. His usual route home was via a bridge over an estuary. When he got to the bridge he asked: 'Are you calling me to walk on water, Lord?' Thinking he heard God say yes, he stepped out and promptly sank. He tried several times, until finally a policeman who had been called by an onlooker concerned about the young man's mental state, stopped him.

This story became an urban legend in YWAM and we all laughed at it. But secretly we wondered whether we could walk on water too. God's ways are not our ways and in today's passage Solomon ponders the gap between human wisdom and God's wisdom 'far off and most profound' (v.24).

Sometimes God may ask you to do something that makes no human sense. One of my own 'walking on water' situations came when I was also in YWAM. My husband and I felt we should go to a conference at the other end of the country. The only problem was we had very little petrol and no money in the bank to buy any. And yet, we both felt God was calling us to go. So, tentatively we packed the car and headed off. About 100 miles into the journey our petrol was running low and we pulled into a fuel station. We didn't have enough money to pay for it, so we checked our bank account. Lo and behold, there was more than enough money to cover the petrol all the way to the conference and back. And then, when we got to the conference, someone had paid our fees too!

God has given us a brain, yes, but sometimes He calls us to listen to our heart instead.

For prayer and reflection

Is God calling You to do something beyond human reason? Ask Him today to confirm this through a trusted Christian friend or leader.

WEEKEND

The Life of Solomon – building the Temple

For Reflection: 1 Chronicles 22

'Now, my son ... may you ... build the house of the LORD ... as he said you would.' (1 Chron. 22:11)

I always felt sorry for David. He was the man who laid everything on the line for God: he endured danger, persecution, exile and public humiliation. Nothing was too much for God to ask David. Yes, he was flawed, and the Bible does not hold back on pointing out his sins, but he sought God with all his heart. And yet, God would not allow him one of his greatest desires: to build a temple for the Lord. This honour fell to his son, Solomon. God said it was because there was 'too much blood on his hands'– which you wouldn't think was fair when he'd repented of his sin (see Apr 6/7). But it could also be interpreted as there was too much 'war' during David's reign. A building project is best conducted in peacetime – and Solomon's reign was characterised by peace. Although disappointed, David did not sulk, but did all he could to help prepare for the building. Have you been denied something by God? Why not choose to help others to 'build' in that area despite your own disappointment?

Optional further reading

The building of the Temple by King Solomon: 1 Kings 5–6; The middle reign of King Solomon: 1 Kings 7–10.

MON **APR 22**

Frustration with authority

Ecclesiastes 8:1–16

'Since a king's word is supreme, who can say to him, "What are you doing?"' (v.4)

As a teenager in the 1980s I attended a Baptist church in South Africa. I was becoming increasingly conscious of the injustice of apartheid and frequently raised the issue with leaders in the church. I noticed the Anglican and Catholic churches admitted people of all races and spoke out against the system. When I pointed this out I was told the reason 'we' didn't was because we were a 'Bible-believing church' and the Bible taught that we should respect and obey our leaders even if we don't always agree with them.

I have seen this teaching used to silence people in the workforce, to justify abuse in schools and to allow spiritual leaders to establish an unhealthy level of control in their congregations. What is so easily forgotten is that leadership should be tempered with justice. People in authority need to act with wisdom and fairness. They need to consider the rights of their 'underlings' to be equal to their own.

Let us not forget that Solomon was a king and it was in his best interest to teach people to obey him. However, he is aware that he too has a responsibility towards his subjects. In verse 9 he mentions men who '[lord] it over others to [their] own hurt'. Then in verse 11, he notes that penal justice needed to be carried out promptly or else people will get frustrated.

I remember as a child going to the authority figures in my life to complain about being bullied. They said I shouldn't tell tales, that I must have done something to provoke it, or sympathised with me, but did not do a single thing to stop it. Is it any wonder people lose respect for authority?

For prayer and reflection

We are instructed in the Bible to respect authority and pray for our leaders. If someone in authority over you is acting unjustly, pray for wisdom to know how to challenge it.

NEXT ISSUE

MAY/JUN 2013

May

WINDS OF GOD

CHRISTINE LEONARD

June

TRANSFORMED BY HIS BEAUTY

ABIDEMI SANUSI

In **May**, Christine Leonard explores the dynamic references to winds in the Bible, encouraging us to co-operate this Pentecost with the wind of the Spirit.

In **June**, Abidemi Sanusi contemplates God's beauty reflected in His glory, grace, creativity and the fullness of the Trinity, challenging us likewise to be beautiful women of God in our everyday lives.

Obtain your copy from CWR, Christian bookshops or your National Distributor. If you would like to take out a subscription, see the order form at the back of these notes.

Also available as ebook/esubscription

TUES **APR 23**

The ultimate **justice**

Ecclesiastes 9:1–12

'All share a common destiny – the righteous and the wicked, the good and the bad ...' (v.2a)

In an episode of *Modern Family*, it's Sunday and Gloria wants the family to go to church. Not being a very religious man, Jay says he would rather play golf. Then Manny, in an act of rebellion, says he wants to go with Jay, his step-dad, while Gloria, broken hearted, goes to church alone.

But Manny is feeling guilty and needs validation from Jay that he has done the right thing. Jay is keen to share with Manny the 'freedom' that comes with a secular world-view. However, he is reluctant to undermine Manny's faith. So when Manny asks Jay if he believes in God he says yes. When Manny asks if he believes in heaven, he says he does. When Manny asks if he believes in hell, he pauses then says he doesn't. When Manny asks who goes to heaven, Jay thinks this is his chance to free the boy from the shackles of organised religion and says 'everyone'. Manny looks frightened and asks, 'Even the robbers and murderers?' 'No, not them,' says Jay. 'Then where do they go if there is no hell?' Jay looks uncertain and says, 'To a different part of heaven.' Manny asks what the 'different part' is called. When Jay doesn't answer Manny calls his mother: 'Is it too late to come to church?'

Who goes where when they die has been the subject of much debate. However, the Bible says two things. There will be a day of judgment for all people (Rev. 20:11–15) and it is through Christ alone that we have eternal life (John 14:6). Centuries before Christ, Solomon may not have known this but he knew that it did matter how you lived your life now, and he was certain that in the end, God's justice would prevail.

For prayer and reflection

Lord, help me to live today as if it is my last day on earth. May I work for the benefit of others and make Your love known. Amen.

Forgotten heroes

Hands up who has heard of Florence Nightingale. Good, most of you. Now hands up who has heard of Mary Seacole. Anyone? Come on, don't be shy ... The chances are the vast majority of you will know about the Lady with the Lamp who headed up a troupe of nurses in the Crimean War, saving countless lives on the battlefield, but unless you have gone out of your way to study 'black history' I doubt you will have heard of her darker-skinned colleague.

Mary Seacole* was born in Jamaica in 1805 of mixed race parentage. Her mother was a nurse and Mary learnt how to treat a variety of tropical ailments as well as the horrific injuries suffered on the sugar plantations. In 1854, after making a name for herself as a travelling nurse in Central America, she went to London, hoping to be included in Florence Nightingale's group. But she was overlooked. Undeterred, she raised the money herself and travelled to the Crimea. She set up a field hospital at her own expense and started treating the wounded: British and Russians. It is said she went onto the battlefield to treat soldiers where they lay while the guns still raged.

She returned to London and was recognised along with Florence Nightingale as one of the great heroes of the war. She even became friends with the royal family and was appointed the Prince of Wales' private masseur. But after her death in 1881, like the poor, wise man in Solomon's story, she was soon forgotten.

Thank God for people like Mary Seacole, who have given all they have to serve others, even if they are not remembered.

*Mary Seacole's autobiography – *Wonderful Adventures of Mrs. Seacole in Many Lands* (London: James Blackwood Paternoster Row, 1857) – can also be read online at http://digital.library.upenn.edu/women/seacole/adventures/adventures.html

Ecclesiastes 9:13–10:4

'Now there lived in that city a man poor but wise, and he saved the city ... But nobody remembered [him].' (v.15)

For prayer and reflection

Today, Lord, may I serve You and love others whether or not anyone notices. Sometimes I wonder if anyone sees what I do. Help me, Lord, to no longer care. Amen.

THURS **APR 25**

Watch your mouth

Ecclesiastes 10:5–20; James 3:9–12

'Words from a wise man's mouth are gracious, but a fool is consumed by his own lips.' (Eccl. 10:12)

I'm writing this about ten months before you will read it. Cast your mind back to the Leveson Enquiry into press standards in the UK. As I cannot see into the future and don't know yet what the full judicial findings will be, I cannot comment on specific individuals. However, what I can say is that I have been struck by the dissection of every word and nuance said, texted or written by each of those appearing before the committee. Did the honourable so-and-so really mean he would give preferential treatment to a particular media organisation when he wrote x, y and z? Did the esteemed so-and-so really not know that 'LOL' meant 'laugh out loud' and not 'lots of love'? I shudder to think what someone might think if they read my emails and texts. Taken out of context, what crimes and misdemeanours might I be accused of? In the digital age, when much of our conversation is now conducted via a keyboard and can be accessed by a third party, what do my words say about me? As Solomon puts it, are they foolish or wise? Not long ago I let off steam in an email to a colleague about another colleague. I thought it was going to be private, but the first colleague responded to me and 'cc'd' the second colleague into it! It was highly embarrassing and I had to do a lot of back-pedalling (and repenting!).

The Bible has much to say about the words we speak. 'With the tongue we praise our Lord and Father, and with it we curse men, who have been made in God's likeness' (James 3:9). So do what I say and not what I do: think before you speak, type or text, as your words will reveal what's really in your heart.

For prayer and reflection

Look at some of the texts and emails you have sent recently. Or if you are not 'digital' think back on what you have said. Were your words wise or foolish?

Bread **upon the waters**

Ecclesiastes 11:1–6

'Cast your bread upon the waters, for after many days you will find it again.' (v.1)

About 17 years ago I was in a place in my life, work and ministry where I had lots of options but was unsure what to do. I needed guidance from God and was terrified I would make the wrong decision. Then one day I was drawn to this passage.

It spoke about two things: being generous with what you already have even if you don't know where your next meal or income will come from (v.2), and not waiting until you know for sure which is the right course of action but rather, trying a number of options to see which will yield a return (v.1) or succeed (v.6). This suggests living a life of generosity, faith and risk and since taking this on board, it is the way I have tried to live my life.

Many people have things they would like to do or think God might be calling them to but are paralysed by uncertainty. Recently, a friend of my husband and I contacted us to ask our advice on a big project he felt might be something from God. It involved buying a large property and setting up a youth camp. Now ordinarily we would advise caution when entering into something with a financial risk. However, this friend has been wanting to set up a youth project for 20 years and every time an opportunity comes around he spends so much time wondering if it is from God and waiting for a 'clear word from the Lord' that it never happens. He is like the person in verse 4 who watches the wind and the clouds so much that he never plants or reaps. So we advised our friend to take a risk and 'sow his seed', then wait to see what God will do. And if it goes wrong? Then God has a plan for that too.

For prayer and reflection

Are you faced with a decision and don't know which is the right way to go? Consider casting your bread upon the waters and waiting to see what the Lord does with it.

WEEKEND

The Life of Solomon – Solomon's women

For reflection: 1 Kings 11:1–14; 14:21–31

'As Solomon grew old, his wives turned his heart after other gods, and his heart was not fully devoted to the LORD ...' (v.4)

What a sad end to a promising life.

Last weekend you may have read of the triumphs of Solomon and his Temple, the awe in which the world held him (resulting in visits from the Queen of Sheba and other dignitaries), his great wisdom and his devotion to 'the name of the Lord' (1 Kings 10:1). Over the last month you have been reading one of his great works of literature and no doubt have dipped in and out of the Proverbs that have given advice to religious and secular people alike over the last three millennia. Yet in one generation, we read of the death knell of David and Solomon's great dynasty when all the treasures of the Temple and palace are plundered and Rehoboam replaces them with mere bronze (14:27). So what went wrong? Solomon had a weakness. Despite being warned against it, he went ahead and married 900 women who worshipped other gods. In his efforts to please them, his heart was drawn away from God. What is your weakness? Have you been warned against it? It's time to take that warning seriously.

Optional further reading

The last years of King Solomon and the failure of his son: 1 Kings 11–14.

It's never too late to start **living**

MON **APR 29**

Ecclesiastes 11:7–12:8

'However many years a man may live, let him enjoy them all.' (11:8a)

I received an email today from a friend. She is a gifted, beautiful woman (on the inside and outside), in her mid forties and at the top of her profession. She is married with a gorgeous young daughter. And yet, she said, she feels like she is drifting to the edges of her life and becoming increasingly invisible. She told me she went into the post office the other day and the teller looked at her intently and said: 'My, you must have been beautiful when you were young.' She is at the time of life when new recruits in her office are young enough to be her children. She said that she no longer has any dreams for herself but that all those she had, she now has for her daughter.

Contrast that with another friend of mine who had her first novel published when she was in her mid seventies. And a lady I met on an Alpha Course who decided to become a Christian and got baptised at 80!

In today's passage we see a man approaching the end of his life and regretting what has been lost. Solomon's advice is wise: 'Remember your Creator in the days of your youth, before the years of trouble come ...' (12:1). But remember Him when you are old too. Consider Sarah and Abraham who upped tent-pegs and travelled to their promised land when they were in their seventies (Gen. 12). Consider Anna the prophetess who frequented the courts of the Temple every day until well into her eighties for the chance to glimpse the Messiah (Luke 2:36–38).

As the years pass, the challenges we face and the dreams we have may change, but they should not dry up. A life with God should fulfil us until the day we die – and beyond!

For prayer and reflection

Lord, let me continue to dream for You and to live for You. Help me let go of the regrets for what was and to embrace what will be. Amen.

TUES **APR 30**

Summing it up

Ecclesiastes 12:9–14

'Now all has been heard; here is the conclusion of the matter; Fear God and keep his commandments ...' (Eccl. 12:13)

The authorship of this passage suddenly changes to third person. It's as if someone found Solomon's book after he died, considered the first ending too depressing, so added something. However, it is more likely that Solomon was adopting a dramatic device of shifting between internal and external narration to give a sense that the 'internal' narrator was an actor in his own play; that he too needs to be judged and assessed.

Ecclesiastes is one man's assessment of a life that has been lived and his judgment of its value. We are now invited to assess that assessment. The 'external' narrator reminds us of all the other things the internal narrator has written and that they are 'upright and true' (v.10) even though it has wearied the body of the writer (and this is a good point at which to ask you to pray for me as at the end of a writing project like this I often feel drained).

The external narrator then sums up the message of the book: fear God and keep His commandments because all you do in your life will be judged and nothing will be hidden. A month ago we learnt that this book is a 'bird's eye view' of life. But perhaps more accurately, it's a 'God's eye view'. As we are invited to see things through God's eyes we can look back over the book and see what has meaning and what does not. We see too that all the accoutrements of life, what we do 'under the sun' – wealth, education, entertainment, relationships etc – are meaningless and have no value in themselves. However, they take on value when our lives are focused primarily on loving, serving and obeying God. And that is the conclusion of it all.

For prayer and reflection

Father God, thank You for what You have taught me through the book of Ecclesiastes. Help me, Lord, to see in my own life what has true meaning and what does not. Amen.